W9-BXT-408

Totally Fierce
Animals

by Lisa M. Herrington

Content Consultant
Robbin Friedman, Children's Librarian
Chappaqua (N.Y.) Library

Reading Consultant
Jeanne M. Clidas, Ph.D.
Reading Specialistt

Children's Press®
An Imprint of Scholastic Inc.

Library of Congress Cataloging-in-Publication Data

Names: Herrington, Lisa M.
Title: Totally fierce animals/by Lisa M. Herrington.
Description: New York, NY: Children's Press, [2017] | Series: Rookie amazing
America | Includes index.
Identifiers: LCCN 2016030335 | ISBN 9780531228968 (library binding) | ISBN
9780531225905 (pbk.)
Subjects: LCSH: Carnivora—Juvenile literature. | Bald eagle—Juvenile literature. |
Rattlesnakes—Juvenile literature. | American bison—Juvenile literature.
Classification: LCC QL737.C2 H357 2017 | DDC 599.7—dc23
LC record available at https://lccn.loc.gov/2016030335

No part of this publication may be reproduced in whole or in part, or stored in a retrieval system,
or transmitted in any form or by any means, electronic, mechanical, photocopying, recording, or
otherwise, without written permission of the publisher. For information regarding permission,
write to Scholastic Inc., Attention: Permissions Department, 557 Broadway, New York, NY 10012.

Produced by Spooky Cheetah Press

© 2017 by Scholastic Inc.

All rights reserved. Published in 2017 by Children's Press, an imprint of Scholastic Inc.

Printed in China 62

SCHOLASTIC, CHILDREN'S PRESS, ROOKIE AMAZING AMERICA™, and associated logos are trademarks
and/or registered trademarks of Scholastic Inc.

1 2 3 4 5 6 7 8 9 10 R 26 25 24 23 22 21 20 19 18 17

Photographs ©: cover: Paul Sawyer/FLPA/Minden Pictures; back cover sky: ooyoo/iStockphoto; back cover main:
David Fleetham/Barcroft India/Barcroft Media/Getty Images; 3 background: Scott Cramer/iStockphoto; 3 top
right: Todd Ryburn Photography/Getty Images; 3 bottom: Matthias Breiter/Minden Pictures; 4: Kathleen Reeder
Wildlife Photography/Getty Images; 5: BirdofPrey/iStockphoto; 6-7 main: Josef Friedhuber/Getty Images; 7
inset: Steven Kazlowski/NPL/Minden Pictures; 8 inset: Mint Images/Art Wolfe/Getty Images; 8 background, 9:
Steven Kazlowski/NPL/Minden Pictures; 10 inset: David Parsons/iStockphoto; 10-11 main: Fuse/Getty Images;
12 background, 13: Tim Fitzharris/Minden Pictures; 12 inset: Matthias Breiter/Minden Pictures; 15 inset:
Brian E. Kushner/Getty Images; 15 main: Todd Ryburn Photography/Getty Images; 16-17: Eastcott Momatiuk/
Getty Images; 18: Maria Dryhout/iStockphoto; 19 main: keydog818/iStockphoto; 19 inset: Ingo Arndt/Minden
Pictures; 20 left inset: Kitch Bain/Shutterstock, Inc.; 20 right inset: Bert de Ruiter/Alamy Images; 20-21 main:
Moelyn Photos/Getty Images; 22-23 sky: IP Galanternik D.U./iStockphoto; 22-23 main: Todd Winner/Stocktrek
Images/Getty Images; 23 inset: Robert Blanchard/iStockphoto; 24-25 main: Franco Banfi/Getty Images; 24
inset: David Fleetham/Barcroft India/Barcroft Media/Getty Images; 26-27 background: Alphotographic/
iStockphoto; 26 top left: Kathleen Reeder Wildlife Photography/Getty Images; 26 top right: Steven Kazlowski/
NPL/Minden Pictures; 26 center left: Fuse/Getty Images; 26 center right: Eastcott Momatiuk/Getty Images;
26 bottom left: Maria Dryhout/iStockphoto; 26 bottom right: Moelyn Photos/Getty Images; 27 top right:
Todd Ryburn Photography/Getty Images; 28-29 background: ooyoo/iStockphoto; 28 main: Michal Ninger/
Shutterstock, Inc.; 29 main: Ryan M/ Bolton/Shutterstock, Inc.; 30 background: Kenneth Canning/iStockphoto;
30 top left: Karine Aigner/Getty Images; 30 bottom: Jeff Rotman/Getty Images; 30 top right: EcoPic/
iStockphoto; 31 center bottom: Joe McDonald/Getty Images; 31 top: Maria Dryhout/iStockphoto; 31 center
top: Eastcott Momatiuk/Getty Images; 31 center: Steven Kazlowski/NPL/Minden Pictures; 31 bottom: Brian E.
Kushner/Getty Images; 32 bottom: Arto Hakola/Getty Images; 32 background: Scott Cramer/iStockphoto; 32
top right: Todd Ryburn Photography/Getty Images.

Maps by Jim McMahon.

Table of Contents

U.S. Range:
Alaska, northern
United States

This gray wolf has teeth as sharp as knives.

Gray wolves are fast and powerful hunters. They live and hunt in groups called packs.

There are lots of fierce animals in the United States. Let's explore some more!

Fierce Fact!

Gray wolves hunt animals as big and strong as elks.

Powerful Predators

Polar bears look cuddly, but they are the largest meat eaters on land. They can weigh almost as much as a small car!

These bears live in the Arctic. That cold, icy land includes parts of Alaska. Polar bears spend most of their lives on sea ice.

U.S. Range:
Arctic

Fierce
Fact!

A polar bear's paw
is larger than a
dinner plate.

Polar bears are **predators**.
A predator is an animal that eats other animals.
Seals are polar bears' favorite food.

Fierce Fact!

A polar bear's nose knows! It can smell a seal on the ice from miles away.

The grizzly bear is another fierce predator. This huge hunter is very quick. A grizzly can run faster than a horse! It catches deer and elk.

Fierce Fact!

Grizzlies have brown fur. As they get older, the tips of their hairs turn white, or grizzled. That is how they got their name.

U.S. Range:
Alaska,
western states

11

You would not want to pet this cat. It is a mountain lion.

Mountain lions are hunters. They quietly stalk deer and other **prey**. Then they attack with a powerful jump. A mountain lion can leap about 15 feet (5 meters) from the ground into a tree.

U.S. Range:
western states, small
population in Florida

Fierce Fact!

Mountain lions
are also known as
cougars, pumas,
and panthers.

American Symbols

This huge bird is a bald eagle. It is taller than a two-year-old kid! The bald eagle is our national bird. It is found only in North America.

A bald eagle likes to feast on fish. It uses its sharp eyesight to spot fish from above. Then it swoops down to catch them with its **talons**. It uses its beak to tear the food apart.

talons

The bald eagle is not really bald. It has white feathers on its head.

The bison is our country's national **mammal**.

Bison may not look fierce, but they can be. These big, shaggy animals have sharp horns. They will charge to protect themselves or their babies. They are also speedy. A bison can outrun the fastest person!

Fierce Fact!

Bison are the heaviest land animals in North America. They can weigh up to 2,000 pounds (907 kilograms). That is about as much as 12 people!

U.S. Range: national parks, private ranches

horns

Surprise Attackers!

Look out! Many animals, like the rattlesnake, sneak up on prey.

Rats, lizards, and other small animals make tasty meals. A rattlesnake uses its **fangs** to poison its prey. Then it swallows its food whole.

fangs

Fierce Fact!

When in danger, a rattlesnake may shake its tail. This warns enemies to stay away. The snake can move its rattle back and forth more than 60 times a second.

Chomp! One of the most dangerous animals in the world is the American alligator.

This predator has powerful jaws and a huge body. It lives in swamps and lakes.

alligator

crocodile

Fierce Fact!

How can you tell an alligator from a crocodile? The secret is in the snout. Alligators have U-shaped mouths and crocs have V-shaped mouths.

Range: southeastern
United States

21

Fierce Fact!

An alligator's jaws are strong enough to crack a turtle's shell.

Is that a log or an alligator? An alligator floating with its head just above water looks like a log. Then it attacks when another animal comes near. Alligators have an appetite for fish, birds, frogs, turtles, and other animals. They can also take down big animals like deer.

fish

Great white sharks swim in our oceans. But they are not looking to attack people. They would rather dine on seals or sea lions.

Great whites swim deep, looking for prey above. Then they shoot up with a burst of speed—and bite!

Whether they are sneaky or speedy, many of America's animals sure are fierce!

U.S. Range:
coastal waters

25

United States

From oceans to mountains, fierce animals live everywhere. Can you find them on the map?

1 gray wolf

2 polar bear

3 grizzly bear

4 American bison

5 rattlesnake

6 American alligator

Washington

Montana **3**

Oregon

Idaho **4**

Nevada

Utah

California

Arizona **5**

Alaska **2**

3

Hawaii

Alaska and Hawaii are not drawn to scale or placed in their proper places.

For Fun: One "fishy" animal in this book has more than 3,000 teeth in many rows. If a tooth falls out, another moves up to replace it. Can you guess which animal it is?

Answer: great white shark

of America

New Hampshire

Michigan

Vermont

Maine

North Dakota

Minnesota

Massachusetts

New York

Wyoming

South Dakota

Wisconsin

Rhode Island

Connecticut

Pennsylvania

New Jersey

Iowa

Ohio

Delaware

Nebraska

Illinois

Indiana

West Virginia

Virginia

Maryland

Washington, D.C. (U.S. capital)

Colorado

Kansas

Missouri

Kentucky

North Carolina

Tennessee

Oklahoma

Arkansas

South Carolina

New Mexico

Alabama

Georgia

Texas

Louisiana

Mississippi

Florida

Compass Rose

North

West ◆ East

South

Which Is Fiercer?

Wolverine

- It lives in Alaska and northwestern states.

- This animal is not a wolf. It looks like a small bear but is related to weasels.

- A wolverine is small but very tough. It may attack animals many times its own size.

- Wolverines often dig into animals' burrows to eat whatever lives inside.

You Decide!

Alligator Snapping Turtle

- This is the largest freshwater turtle in North America.

- It is found in southern lakes, rivers, and swamps.

- This turtle has a secret weapon—a wiggly, wormlike part on its tongue.

- With its mouth open, the turtle lies still in the water. A fish tries to grab what it thinks is a worm. Then the turtle slams its mouth shut.

Guess Who?

This creature has eight legs and is related to spiders. It can grab and crush insects with its claws. It can also sting prey with its tail. Ouch! Which creature is it?

claws

A.
crab

claws

B.
scorpion

claws

C.
lobster

Answer: B. scorpion

Glossary

- **fangs** (FANGS): long, pointed teeth

- **mammal** (MAM-uhl): warm-blooded animal that gives birth to live young and produces milk to feed them

- **predators** (PRED-uh-turs): animals that hunt other animals for food

- **prey** (PRAY): animal hunted by another animal for food

- **talons** (TAL-uhns): sharp claws of a bird of prey, such as the bald eagle

Index

Facts for Now

Visit this Scholastic Web site for more information on Fierce Animals:

www.factsfornow.scholastic.com

Enter the keywords Fierce Animals

About the Author

Lisa M. Herrington loves to write for children. She lives in Trumbull, Connecticut with her husband, daughter, and two not-so-fierce goldfish.